The Order of Things

Barbara L. Webb

rourkeeducationalmedia.com

www.rourkeeducationalmedia.com

PHOTO CREDITS: Cover, Page 3,4,5,6,7: © pagadesign, oariff, millsrymer; Title Page: © Joshua Hodge Photography; Page 8, 9,10,11,12,13,14,15,16,17,18,19,20,21,22,23: © Eric Gevaert, Joshua Hodge Photography

Edited by Precious McKenzie

Cover design by Teri Intzegian
Interior design by Tara Raymo

Library of Congress PCN Data

The Order of Things / Barbara L. Webb.
(Little World Math)
ISBN 978-1-61810-074-0 (hard cover)
ISBN 978-1-61810-207-2 (soft cover)
Library of Congress Control Number: 2011944384

Rourke Educational Media
Printed in the United States of America,
North Mankato, Minnesota

rourkeeducationalmedia.com

customerservice@rourkeeducationalmedia.com • PO Box 643328 Vero Beach, Florida 32964

An order gives places to the things in a line.

Find the first one and count. You'll do fine!

1st

The green car is first in the order, it's true.

The red car has a place in the order too.

Start with the green car and count
to the red. 1...2...and 3, 4, 5.

Now you've got it!

Do you know how to say the order of the runners in this race today?

Orange shirt, she's first.

1st

Green shirt is second.

2nd

Blue shirt is in third.

3rd

Does he have a chance to win it?

What's this?

Green shirt slows down and takes a break.

Blue is now in second place.

It's his lucky day!

1st

2nd

When you need to order things, now you know the way!

Index

Websites

www.primarygames.com/squigly/start.htm

www.ngfl-cymru.org.uk/vtc/ordinal_numbers/eng/Introduct/

www.watchknowlearn.org/Category.aspx?CategoryID=5931

About the Author

Barbara Webb lives on the 8th floor of a building on the south side of Chicago where the street names are numbered from 8th Street all the way up to 138th Street! She is the author of several books on math, science, and history for kids.

Ask The Author!
www.rem4students.com

24